UNSER KAMPF

BOOKS BY LOUIS DANIEL BRODSKY

Poetry

Five Facets of Myself   (1967)* (1995)

The Easy Philosopher   (1967)* (1995)

"A Hard Coming of It" and Other Poems   (1967)* (1995)

The Foul Rag-and-Bone Shop   (1967)* (1969, exp.)* (1995, exp.)

Points in Time   (1971)* (1995) (1996)

Taking the Back Road Home   (1972)* (1997) (2000)

Trip to Tipton and Other Compulsions   (1973)* (1997)

"The Talking Machine" and Other Poems   (1974)* (1997)

Tiffany Shade   (1974)* (1997)

Trilogy: A Birth Cycle   (1974) (1998)

Cold Companionable Streams   (1975)* (1999)

Monday's Child   (1975) (1998)

Preparing for Incarnations   (1975)* (1976, exp.) (1999) (1999, exp.)

The Kingdom of Gewgaw   (1976) (2000)

Point of Americas II   (1976) (1998)

La Preciosa   (1977) (2001)

Stranded in the Land of Transients   (1978) (2000)

The Uncelebrated Ceremony of Pants-Factory Fatso   (1978) (2001)

Birds in Passage   (1980) (2001)

Résumé of a Scrapegoat   (1980) (2001)

Mississippi Vistas: Volume One of *A Mississippi Trilogy*   (1983) (1990)

You Can't Go Back, Exactly   (1988, two eds.) (1989) (2003, exp.)

The Thorough Earth   (1989)

Four and Twenty Blackbirds Soaring   (1989)

Falling from Heaven: Holocaust Poems of a Jew and a Gentile *(with William Heyen)*   (1991)

Forever, for Now: Poems for a Later Love   (1991)

Paper-Whites for Lady Jane: Poems of a Midlife Love Affair   (1992)* (1995)

Mistress Mississippi: Volume Three of *A Mississippi Trilogy*   (1992)

A Gleam in the Eye: Volume One of *The Seasons of Youth*   (1992) (2009)

Gestapo Crows: Holocaust Poems   (1992)

The Third Year's a Charm: Later-Love Poems   (1993)*

The Capital Café: Poems of Redneck, U.S.A.   (1993)

Disappearing in Mississippi Latitudes: Volume Two of *A Mississippi Trilogy*   (1994)

Variations on a Love Theme: Poems for Janie   (1995)*

A Mississippi Trilogy: A Poetic Saga of the South   (1995)*

The Complete Poems of Louis Daniel Brodsky: Volume One, 1963–1967
   (edited by Sheri L. Vandermolen)   (1996)

Three Early Books of Poems by Louis Daniel Brodsky, 1967–1969: *The Easy Philosopher,*
"*A Hard Coming of It" and Other Poems*, and *The Foul Rag-and-Bone Shop*
(edited by Sheri L. Vandermolen)   (1997)

The Eleventh Lost Tribe: Poems of the Holocaust   (1998)

Toward the Torah, Soaring: Poems of the Renascence of Faith   (1998)

Voice Within the Void: Poems of *Homo supinus*   (2000)

The Swastika Clock: Holocaust Poems   (2000)*   (2011)

Rabbi Auschwitz: Poems of the Shoah   (2000)*   (2009)

Shadow War: A Poetic Chronicle of September 11 and Beyond, Volume One   (2001)   (2004)

The Complete Poems of Louis Daniel Brodsky: Volume Two, 1967–1976
(edited by Sheri L. Vandermolen)   (2002)

Shadow War: A Poetic Chronicle of September 11 and Beyond, Volume Two   (2002)   (2004)

Shadow War: A Poetic Chronicle of September 11 and Beyond, Volume Three   (2002)   (2004)

Shadow War: A Poetic Chronicle of September 11 and Beyond, Volume Four   (2002)   (2004)

Shadow War: A Poetic Chronicle of September 11 and Beyond, Volume Five   (2002)   (2004)

Regime Change: Poems of America's Showdown with Iraq, Volume One   (2002)*

Heavenward   (2003)*

Regime Change: Poems of America's Showdown with Iraq, Volume Two   (2003)*

Regime Change: Poems of America's Showdown with Iraq, Volume Three   (2003)*

The Location of the Unknown: Shoah Poems   (2004)*

The Complete Poems of Louis Daniel Brodsky: Volume Three, 1976–1980
(edited by Sheri L. Vandermolen)   (2004)

Peddler on the Road: Days in the Life of Willy Sypher   (2005)

Combing Florida's Shores: Poems of Two Lifetimes   (2006)

Showdown with a Cactus: Poems Chronicling the Prickly Struggle Between the Forces
of Dubya-ness and Enlightenment, 2003–2006   (2006)

A Transcendental Almanac: Poems of Nature   (2006)

Once upon a Small-Town Time: Poems of America's Heartland   (2007)

Still Wandering in the Wilderness: Poems of the Jewish Diaspora   (2007)

The World Waiting to Be: Poems About the Creative Process   (2008)

The Complete Poems of Louis Daniel Brodsky: Volume Four, 1981–1985
(edited by Sheri L. Vandermolen)   (2008)

Unser Kampf: Poems of the Final Solution   (2008)*   (2013)

Dine-Rite: Breakfast Poems   (2008)

Rien Sans Amour: Love Poems for Jane   (2009)*

By Leaps and Bounds: Volume Two of *The Seasons of Youth*   (2009)

At Water's Edge: *Poems of Lake Nebagamon*, Volume One   (2010)

Seizing the Sun and Moon: Volume Three of *The Seasons of Youth*   (2010)

At Dock's End: *Poems of Lake Nebagamon*, Volume Two   (2011)

Poetry (continued)

In the Liberation Camps: Poems of the Endlösung   (2011)*
Just Ours: *Love Passages with Linda*, Volume One   (2011)
Hopgrassers and Flutterbies: Volume Four of *The Seasons of Youth*   (2011)
Saul and Charlotte: Poems Commemorating a Father and Mother   (2011)
Each Other: *Love Passages with Linda*, Volume Three   (2011)*
Seiwa-en: Poems in the Japanese Garden   (2012)*
At Shore's Border: *Poems of Lake Nebagamon*, Volume Three   (2012)
Our Time: *Love Passages with Linda*, Volume Two   (2012)
We Two: *Love Passages with Linda*, Volume Four   (2012)*
You, Me: *Love Passages with Linda*, Volume Five   (2012)*
Burnt Offerings of the Thousand-Year Reich: Holocaust Poems   (2012)*
Eying Wider Horizons: Volume Five of *The Seasons of Youth*   (2012)

Bibliography (coedited with Robert Hamblin)

Selections from the William Faulkner Collection of Louis Daniel Brodsky: A Descriptive Catalogue   (1979)
Faulkner: A Comprehensive Guide to the Brodsky Collection: Volume I, The Biobibliography   (1982)
Faulkner: A Comprehensive Guide to the Brodsky Collection: Volume II, The Letters   (1984)
Faulkner: A Comprehensive Guide to the Brodsky Collection: Volume III, *The De Gaulle Story*   (1984)
Faulkner: A Comprehensive Guide to the Brodsky Collection: Volume IV, *Battle Cry*   (1985)
Country Lawyer and Other Stories for the Screen by William Faulkner   (1987)
Faulkner: A Comprehensive Guide to the Brodsky Collection: Volume V, Manuscripts and Documents   (1989)
Stallion Road: A Screenplay by William Faulkner   (1989)

Biography

William Faulkner, Life Glimpses   (1990)

Fiction

Between Grief and Nothing *(novel)*   (1964)*
Between the Heron and the Wren *(novel)*   (1965)*
"Dink Phlager's Alligator" and Other Stories   (1966)*
The Drift of Things *(novel)*   (1966)*
Vineyard's Toys *(novel)*   (1967)*
The Bindle Stiffs *(novel)*   (1968)*
Yellow Bricks *(short fictions)*   (1999)

Fiction (continued)

Catchin' the Drift o' the Draft *(short fictions)*   (1999)

This Here's a Merica *(short fictions)*   (1999)

Leaky Tubs *(short fictions)*   (2001)

Rated Xmas *(short fictions)*   (2003)

Nuts to You! *(short fictions)*   (2004)

Pigskinizations *(short fictions)*   (2005)

With One Foot in the Butterfly Farm *(short fictions)*   (2009)

Getting to Unknow the Neighbors *(short fictions)*   (2010)

Memoir

The Adventures of the Night Riders, Better Known as the Terrible Trio
 (with Richard Milston)   (1961)*

---

* *Unpublished*

UNSER KAMPF
Poems of the Final Solution

BY
LOUIS DANIEL BRODSKY

An imprint of Time Being Press
St. Louis, Missouri

Copyright © 2013 by Louis Daniel Brodsky

All rights reserved under International and Pan-American Copyright Conventions. No part of this book shall be reproduced in any form (except by reviewers for the public press) without written permission from the publisher:

> Time Being Books®
> 10411 Clayton Road
> St. Louis, Missouri 63131

Time Being Books® is an imprint of Time Being Press®, St. Louis, Missouri.

Time Being Press® is a 501(c)(3) not-for-profit corporation.

Time Being Books® volumes are printed on acid-free paper.

ISBN 978-1-56809-197-6 (paperback)
ISBN 978-1-56809-198-3 (electronic)

Library of Congress Cataloging-in-Publication Data:

Brodsky, Louis Daniel.
  Unser Kampf : poems of the Final Solution / by Louis Daniel Brodsky.
    — First edition.
    pages cm
  ISBN 978-1-56809-197-6 (paperback : acid-free paper) — ISBN 978-1-56809-198-3 (electronic)
  1. Title. II. Title: Poems of the Final Solution.
  PS3552.R623U57 2013
  811'.54—dc23

2013010120

Cover design by Jeff Hirsch
Book design and typesetting by Trilogy M. Mattson

Manufactured in the United States of America
First Edition, first printing (2013)

ACKNOWLEDGMENTS

Certain poems in this book have appeared, in different versions, in the following publications: *European Judaism* ("Late"), *Midstream* ("Ask the Rain" and "Tonight, You Sleep"), and *Shirim* ("Not Enough Information").

CONTENTS

I: Survivors

The Healing *19*

Failure *20*

The Heart of Nowhere *21*

Mist *22*

The Bottom of the Box *23*

Holocaust Poet *25*

Ask the Rain *26*

Betrunken *27*

The Lesser Evil *28*

Quarry *29*

Weight Loss *30*

Retribution *32*

Death as a Way of Life *33*

II: Lunacy

The Mirror *37*

Windup Jew *38*

Good Fences Make Good Sheep *39*

Iridescence *41*

Late *42*

An Exceptional Night on the Graveyard Shift *43*

The Ravine *44*

Mein Kampf, by Satan *45*

The Poet Who Wrote Free-Verse Tattoos *47*

Candle *48*

The Black Attic *49*

III: Perished

Tonight, You Sleep   53
Hindsight   54
The Deep   55
Surviving Nightmare   56
Pinching Myself   57
Everyjew   58
Pigeon Shit   59
Anesthesia   60
A Meaning of Life   61
Dark Lovers   62
He and You   63
Beyond Sleep   65
I Did   66
The Pattern   67
Haven't Yet   68

IV: These Days

Experiments   71
The Victim Who Survived His Nonexistence   72
Holocaust Contest   73
Not Enough Information   74
Oskar Selbstmord   76
Monopoly   77
Unpronounceable   78
Yesterday and Yesterday and Yesterday   79
Latrine   81
Risen Grace   82
Vacuum   83

UNSER KAMPF

I
Survivors

I: SURVIVORS

The Healing

When he finally returned home,
From his journey around the world beyond his fears,
He was drained, deranged, estranged, mind-blown, lonely.

After all, undertaking a crusade of such magnitude
Required the guts of an audacious man of faith,
Someone willing to place his head in the jaws of an alligator

And wait for the beast to snap it off,
While he prayed for a deus ex machina *in absentia*
To save him from sifting to the bottom of the cosmic food chain.

For years, he recuperated, as best he could, out in life's barn,
Competing, with the chickens, pigs, horses, and cows,
For a patch of unsullied straw

On which to sleep away the benign, ambiguous hours,
Allowing his psychic wounds to seal their fates,
Before setting off, again, for terror incognita.

How many days, decades, eons he languished there,
He couldn't begin to say,
Nor could the chickens, pigs, horses, and cows.

All he knew was that his recuperation was salubrious,
Because, eventually, anxiety and abject horror forsook him,
Left his essence to survive by eating barnyard feces,

Which, except on a few really awful lightning-storm nights,
Failed to remind him of his time in the camps,
Gave him a feeling of anesthetic healing and quietus.

Failure

When all else fails,
There's always that one final fallback position,
The spirit's last bastion, its safety net: death.

When things get so bleak, desperate,
That life loses its luster, its swift kick in the butt,
Lacks even the status of third-class citizenship,

One can, with the slightest bit of beginner's luck,
Take the necessary steps
Toward requisitioning the basic components.

After all, how difficult can it really be,
Finding escape routes, trapdoors,
Taking the proverbial hike, buying the farm?

Needless to say, that's a rhetorical question
Which I'm too highly well qualified
Not to answer, in my own good time.

For days, months, I've pondered the outcome,
Weighed the ad hoc pros and cons,
Meditated on the best stratagems.

And don't think I've not studied demises —
Aunts', uncles', cousins', brothers', sisters', parents' —
To facilitate taking my failure away.

When you're feeling low, in the town dumps,
And there's no other recourse
But to let the black crows have their way,

Peck what's left of your ravaged soul,
All you can do is submit.
It's then, only then, that the end commences,

Thoughts of calling it quits really set in,
Convince you that the right decision
Is to terminate the journey.

Suddenly, you sense what you have to do:
Go home, get in bed, naked,
And, with a sigh of relief, bite down on death.

I: SURVIVORS

The Heart of Nowhere

For the past few weeks, months, years, decades,
Ever since I first became aware
That my soul lost its way, went missing,

All I've been able to accomplish
Is getting out of bed, each disorienting morning,
Surviving the intervening hours of enervating ennui,

In my mind's displaced-persons camp,
Located somewhere in the heart of nowhere,
Before crawling back between the sheets, each evening.

It's been this way, second to minute to hour,
Seemingly forever . . . forever after . . .
After what I've never been able to escape,

Other than in my fanciful reveries,
When I allow my imagination to return to its youth,
Before the ghostly, dust-mote deportations —

My *cheder* days in Berlin
(Or was it Warsaw, Vienna, Budapest, Prague?),
Devoted to studying the Torah, Talmud, Zohar,

With dreams of becoming God's voice to His people,
A wise man, *kohen*, kind and compassionate rabbi,
The pride of my city, ghetto, cattle car, death camp.

And then it was done; and then it all passed,
That vast, cataclysmic aberration of human delusion,
In which genocide took center stage,

Mimed its *Mein Kampf* lines, to perfection,
Goose-strutted its petty, spit-shined-jackboot pace,
And I was left waking and sleeping, sleeping and waking,

Trying to locate my soul, in the land of the unknown,
Long after the last ashes from the furnaces
Settled in Brooklyn, Miami, Jerusalem, Montreal,

The last vapors from the Zyklon B showers
Sifted into the *mikvah*s at Masada, the caves of Qumran,
The crevices in the Kotel, the grottoes at Yad Vashem.

Mist

The demarcation of weeks into days means nothing,
Nothing to you, anyway,
Since time is just a serialization of changelessness

And you consider yourself but a piece of straw
In a frenzied eagle's beak,
Destined to line its nest, beyond forever.

Time is as irrelevant to your existence
As summer and winter, left and right,
Memory and forgetting, life and demise.

For all intents and purposeless pretenses,
You can barely distinguish light from darkness,
Such is the mist in which your oblivious spirit operates.

That you're a recluse is obvious enough.
You can't even recognize yourself
In a mirror scribbled with your name, in Gothic script,

You, a spectral leftover of something too horrific
Even for God to resurrect from humanity's ashpits —
History's invisible misfit,

Issue of Yiddish-speaking Polish ciphers
Spit out of evil's toothbrush-mustached,
Schnapps-fouled mouth,

Shipped off to the matzah bakery,
To propagate the zombie population,
Destined to line the nest of the crooked-wing eagle.

At eighty-eight, you have some right to complain.
After all, had you just been gassed,
The past sixty years would have spared you this death.

The Bottom of the Box

I have moments, days, months, decades, eons
When I feel as though, inescapably,
I'm the worthless prize at the bottom of a Cracker Jack box,

God's poster child for humiliation, degradation, shame,
Mortality's role model
For all felonies and misdemeanors inflicted on the heart,

An all-too-human being,
Incapable of Abrahamic or Homeric deeds of heroism,
Acts of self-effacing austerity, nobility,

An uncommonly common man,
Perhaps not at all unlike precrucified Jesus the Jew,
When he was an anonymous Nazarene carpenter.

Then again and again, tomorrows on end,
I have seconds, hours, weeks, years, millenniums
When I'm not even the booby prize at the 4-H fair,

For the five-uddered cow or the six-legged pig
That fails to garner a single vote of confidence
From a *minyan* of blind, deaf, and dumb judges,

And when, no matter to which Space Shuttle I'm assigned,
The heat of atmospheric reentry
Penetrates my shield tiles and vaporize my bones,

Scatter my ashes, across Texas's desolate grasslands,
Where cattle with adventitious thalidomide limbs
Graze amidst other beasts branded with swastikas.

Tonight, I meditate on my lot in life and afterlife,
Trying to gain a less insane overview
Of my space at the bottom of the Cracker Jack box

Clack-clacking toward Auschwitz, Chelmno, Sobibor —
A cattle car hauling ten-horned, seven-headed ghetto Jews
To Revelation's ghastly Golgotha depot, abattoir.

And that's imprecisely why
I have bad and blacker seasons, periods, passages, spans
When I'm addled by the future of my past.

If only I could make all of it go away —
The Cracker Jack box, the livestock, the shuttles —
I would, as a final solution to my problems.

Holocaust Poet

Tonight, at seventy-seven and counting methodically,
Here you are, again, in an empty café,
Penning yet another poem about the Holocaust.

You're a rickety old bag of arthritic bones,
A lonely so-and-so nobody, mired in your fate,
Bringing up the rear of your rainy-day parade,

Which has stuttered down your heart's Main Street
For six decades, if not, in reality, your entire life . . .
And you're still obsessed with writing an outsider's verse.

Why, night after night, in your cups,
Do you feel so possessive of all those who were killed?
Could it be that you were one of them?

Ask the Rain

How could it have taken tonight's rain showers
Sixty-five years
To find my shadowy silhouette slipping through the trees,

Trees which, for the past half-century, at least,
Have concealed me from grief's argenteous spirits,
Protected me from death's saber teeth?

Could it be that I eluded the clouds' storm troops
Simply by pure fortuitousness,
A sheer matter of simple, godless probability?

Or was it just a case of mistaken Jewish identity
That accounted for my unexplainable escape
From the roll call that devoured Europe's 1940s?

How can I exhume adequate words, appropriate phrases,
To express my ineffable perplexity?
I don't have an answer as to why I'm still breathing

Or whether being alive is better than dying might have been,
In that time of spiritual rot,
When decent Germans turned into demons,

Poltergeists who, once upon a civilized time,
Composed symphonies, concertos, sonatas, for the gods,
Created poems and paintings, dreamed millennial Reichs.

All I know is that in these days of my late eighties,
I'm very sensitive to the rain.
Tonight's drops remind me of bleeding glass.

Could it be that Kristallnacht never happened, never passed,
And that those trees forming the forest beyond my soul
Never sprouted, never provided me shelter,

That, in reality, I failed to survive the last sixty-five years,
Expired with the rest of my family, my people?
Ask the rain. Maybe it can tell you why I'm still here.

I: SURVIVORS

Betrunken

Day after day after day,
The Gestapo were out in conspicuous force,
Patrolling the *Strassen*, *Bierhallen*, *Grünanlagen*,

Searching for political and religious dissidents,
Anarchists, and degenerate artists —
Painters, poets, jazz musicians in the Negro mode.

You, being nothing but a drunken bum,
Wearing an armband of impunity (your stench),
Were a person of inconsequence to them.

Every day was the same crazy masquerade —
Mad chases, captures, escapes, ghettoizations,
Incarcerations, deportations, exterminations.

From your bird's-eye vantage in the gutter,
Too numb to whisper your condolences,
You bore witness to depredation's human comedy.

Throughout Berlin's Nazi scourge,
They never had a clue as to your Orthodox Judaism,
That you were descended of *koben*s and sofers,

Never thought to look for you,
Hiding in your attic of inebriation
Or deep in dipsomania's sewer system.

And yet there you lay, squalid, pathetic,
In plain view of every uniformed god
Who prowled the sidewalks, hungry for prey,

Shamefully shitfaced, disgraceful, benign,
Not worth the cost to ship you off to the camps,
Had they known your identity.

Then your once-beloved city was overrun
With Russians and Americans —
A chaos of liberated . . . liberated *what*? Not Jews.

Not Jews, except for you, that is, the town drunk,
Who'd never had a drink in his life
But managed to stay *betrunken* for a decade.

The Lesser Evil

From some place far back in his brain,
Sounds stranger than any he'd ever experienced
Emanated, in enervating cacophony.

No matter how rigorously he strained,
In his enfeebled tries, to identify the droning din,
All he could muster was a puzzling *nothing*.

And yet, for days, years, his earthly eternity
(Such as it was, for his survivor's soul),
That moaning, bellowing persisted —

A plague of cranial tinnitus,
Distracting him from happiness,
Exacerbating his melancholy, his chronic sadness.

Always, in the background, those beleaguered sounds,
Low-pitched, plangent, plaintive,
They followed him, like loonies in a mental ward,

Threatening to destabilize his viability as a human,
A productive member of a free society
That had accepted him, after the Nazi atrocities,

A democracy that had bequeathed him,
Ungrudgingly, in its enlightened benignity,
A place to live, if not prosper, without fear,

Which really wasn't all that well and good,
Since he couldn't expunge those hysterical sounds,
Following him around, day in, night out,

Through his decades of repatriation,
His attempt to become a whole person again,
Despite having lost his family, in Berlin's memory.

Even when his pauper's spirit was laid to rest,
In a plot provided by his adopted temple,
It still, on entering the worm-squirming, soggy ground,

Heard those afflicting bellows and moans,
Emanating so far back, in his defunct brain,
That death seemed the lesser of the two evils.

I: SURVIVORS

Quarry

Another blustery February Monday morning
Trundles and trudges down winter's dismal corridors,
From somewhere above, somewhere north of here.

I bundle up, against the bristling black winds,
And enter dawn's cacophony,
Like a new recruit dumped off at boot camp.

I try to focus, go about my business-as-usual,
Accept destiny's duties, with discipline and respect,
To prove that I'm not a quitter.

Yet fate couldn't care less about me,
A lowly buck private
In humanity's ragtag, mercenary army reserve.

I wait for orders from above or northern headquarters,
But only interminable waiting speaks to me,
Informs me of what I'll be expected to do: nothing.

Within hours, days, I'm taken to a barracks,
Where I'm outfitted in a striped uniform,
Issued a shovel and pick and bucket,

Led, with a motley of shadows, dreams, fears,
To the head of a craggy path
At the upper edge of a ravine, made to descend.

Days, weeks later, I reach the quarry's cratered floor,
Begin swinging my pick, thrusting my shovel
Into ash, bones, rotting corpses.

Suddenly, I know what the bucket is for:
The missed pocket and wrist watches, fobs,
The eyeglasses, gold fillings, wedding rings, coins.

This blustery Monday seems so many Februarys ago.
If only they'd stop dragging me out of sleep,
Forcing me into depression — history's death pit.

Weight Loss

It took him a little more than a year and a half
To accomplish the desired effect:
Climbing inside the skin of an invisible man.

Why he set himself such a grotesque goal,
Even he, at first, was hard-pressed to explain.
All he knew was that he felt compelled to do so,

Almost as though it were a religious rite of passage
Or, if not, a matter of psychic urgency —
One of those things people do that's not just for the hell of it.

Whatever evil or guilt was responsible for his resolve,
He set about pushing his plate away, at the table,
Gradually taking fewer and fewer bites,

Initially seeing meals as rewards he wasn't entitled to,
For his having failed at this or that innocuous task,
Later, as being tainted with toxic pesticides,

And, in the final stages, as having been laced with Zyklon B,
By cooks (he ate all his meals out)
Conspiring to do him in (his Jewishness was a dead giveaway).

In due time, his pounds shed *him*,
Shunned him, as if in a collective rebuke,
Reduced him, physically, from a robust human being

To a stick figure.
From the beginning of his diminution,
Through the transitional stages of his dismantlement,

To the denouement of his total transmogrification,
A process of jettisoning 140 of his 200 pounds,
He became emaciated, razor-thin, skeletal, a wraith.

At a stark sixty pounds, he felt an eerie exhilaration,
In returning to that numbing emptiness he'd experienced,
That insensate moribundity of the barely living,

Which stalked him, for more than two years,
When he was a prisoner at Auschwitz-Birkenau-Buna,
Before being liberated, by the Americans, in 1945 . . .

I: SURVIVORS

In returning to those dire privations he'd survived,
As if not to do so, once, before he died,
Would be to violate a promise he'd made, in the camps,

Never to let himself forget,
Substitute complacency and excess, for abstinence.
At sixty pounds, he could appreciate life, to the fullest.

Retribution

Lay me to rest, you foul-breathing demons!
Do the best you can to silence me,
And I promise you, by the stars above, ghosts below,

I'll come back to haunt your bones,
Force you to account for your sins,
Make you pay for your scrofulous atrocities, tenfold,

Not with the prospect of absolution, salvation,
Certainly not resurrection!
For your gross malignity, I'll sacrifice your evil lives!

Bury me, you barbaric sons-of-bitches,
And watch me rise, from the grave's fear-soaked embrace,
Death's grotesque clutches, to exact retribution!

Watch your backs, you wraithful scourges!
I harbor such terrible animus toward you
That even Armageddon couldn't annihilate my rage!

And if, in the end, out of intimidation,
You decide to spare me, beware nonetheless!
I'll hunt you down, you bastards,

You who've threatened me, with abominations beyond belief!
I'll rip you limb from limb, burn you alive,
In my memory's eternal furnaces!

Death as a Way of Life

Arguably, admittedly, I have an obsession with death.
OK, now it's finally out.
So much for "don't ask, don't tell." The truth is moot.

You could, conceivably, classify my fascination as a fixation,
A perverse preoccupation with demise, if you choose.
I suggest you see it as a rite of passage

Old age undertakes, of its own volition,
By virtue of living long enough to be able to look back
Without flinching, suffering panic attacks,

As a diehard acrophobic might be able to look down
While walking a steel girder of a skyscraper
Reaching its eighty-fifth story, above Manhattan,

Asking himself what possibly possessed him
To step out on life's unforgiving edge,
On a lark, a whim, daring death to blow him off . . .

Undertakes when the end of life is a given,
A foregone conclusion to a nonrecurring delusion,
An immutable testament to mutability, decease, decay.

I myself, as a voice of one, at most or at least,
Decline to accept the end of me, anyway,
If not Faulknerian man, humanity at large, the planet

Indeed I do. I will not only endure and prevail
Because I have a puny, inexhaustible voice
But because I have a spirit, a soul, capable of chutzpah,

A Diasporan capacity to rise above tsuris,
Anti Semitic, Hitlerian, *Übermensch* hubris
That would consign my pariah's heritage to the ovens,

My faculty for compassion, pity, sacrifice, endurance
To Madjanek, Treblinka, Auschwitz-Birkenau-Buna —
Indeed, I will. I'm immortal.

So, naturally, you ask about my obsession with death.
What more can I say? I'll tell you.
I worship it.

Since oppression is all I've ever known,
I find that death is an abiding, comforting presence.
How otherwise could I endure life's infinite atrocities?

II
Lunacy

The Mirror

When I peer, obliquely, into the mirror behind my mind,
I see a black triceratops, brandishing its three horns,
Charging me, from the dark contours of my heart.

I try to hide behind invisibly clustered trees,
But the creature tramples them
And, goring me, heaves my corpse over its haunches,

Leaves me bleeding, at the edge of a shallow grave
Filled with bleaching bones . . .
Bones that yet seem to be shivering, moaning,

As though they're freezing in the 120 degree heat . . .
Bones that appear, by the way they welcome my spirit,
To know me — kindred spirits, you might say.

Why I stand before this horrific mirror so often,
As if participating in a pagan rite,
Could be a symptom of some metastasizing madness

That's attached itself to the prisms of my transfixed psyche,
An addiction to pain and grieving and death,
Much like a vampire's need for human blood, to stay alive.

Or maybe the reason I stare into this sadistic glass
Is to satisfy its black triceratops's urge
To stir up the past, hurl more bones into the shallow grave,

Knowing, as I do, that escaping its ferocity is impossible,
Verboten by the god of reflections,
Whose mirror of years holds me thrall, in its memory.

Windup Jew

The three ninety-degree turns he took to the right,
With the jaunty imprecision
Of a 1940s German tin windup toy,

Brought him back around to the beginning,
That space from which he'd strayed
When his spring was first torqued to its tightest.

In a shuddering, frenetic spasm,
His mechanism shattered like a grenade,
Scattering his clattering parts, leaving them catawampus.

No one, for thousands of miles,
Heard the abrupt eruption,
Or, if they did, they mistook it for a toilet flushing.

When authorities finally arrived on the scene,
The weed-choked crater
His demise had gouged out of the clay terrain

Was invisible even to the experienced eye.
Only one trace of what he was remained, nearby:
A charred shard of his cog-work heart,

Which still bore, on its blood-rusty surface,
Five faint numbers.
The inspectors erased them with battery acid.

Good Fences Make Good Sheep

The sheep leaping fences separating reality from sleep
Were, deceptively, electrified,
So as to shock me, literally, if I dared escape.

Oh, please excuse the convoluted logic of my mind.
I meant the *fences* were charged, not the *woolly creatures*.
Surely you knew this, though, or you didn't, I think.

Anyway, as I was so ineffectually attempting to say,
The fences cordoning off my dream, from freedom,
Could as easily have been Nazi shepherds and sheep,

Given their predisposition toward murder
(Which had possessed their collective psyche,
From the dawn of the Huns, Vandals, and Visigoths),

Their prodigiously systematic preoccupation with killing,
Performed, first, as animal-sacrifice rites to the gods,
Evolving, gradually, through the Dark and Middle Ages,

To the liquidation of Martin Luther's vermin-Jews,
By the National Socialist German Workers Party,
Preaching racial purity for the thousand-year Reich.

Oh, shut me up! Force me to leave off this drivel.
Bring me back to those fleecy sheep,
Those lambs of God, revered by the Universal Church,

If only for their having bequeathed its first-century fathers
The one Jew worthy of crucifixion and resurrection,
By virtue of his vision of eternal salvation.

Personally, I couldn't give a mad-sheep-disease shit
About those barbaric Hitlers, Himmlers, Görings, Bormanns,
Goebbelses, Heydrichs, Eichmanns, Ribbentrops, Blobels,

Who did their historical bits to guarantee humanity
That it would never tear down their fences guarding slaughter,
Shake their faith in baby-Jesus lambs sleeping in mangers,

Their belief in the necessity of exterminating Jew boys and girls
Before they could leap electrified fences, infect the flocks
Of Aryan Helmuts and Helgas, Hanses and Heidis,

Dreaming of making the world safe from kike-lice
Crawling, like people, in *shtetl*s, cities, ghettos,
Who might fail to sympathize with their genocidal blessings.

Iridescence

One day, long ago in the future,
You would materialize as a red-white-and-black dragonfly,
Beating your netted, iridescent wings

As if lifting in the glorious ascension of Lord Nada,
Pope Millennial Reich, in disguise.
What a strange insectile creature you were, are.

Ah, there occurs, once again,
That very oblique, sinister allusion to a madman,
A bug not in the manner of Gregor Samsa;

Quite the paradoxical contrary,
A spirit skimming and hovering, ever so evanescently,
Over a perpetually smoldering, putrescent pyre,

A beautifully conceived savior of the confused masses,
Saying your High Masses of *Heil Hitler*s
To the Eucharist-Jews you're gnawing, in the quicklime pits.

That, in the long-ago forever, you were, are, a flying dragon
Is the stuff of fables, myth, history of the ages,
A once-in-a-thousand-year incarnation of holy evil,

Capable of making the universe a better place
For tyrants, cannibals, barbarians, and psycho-sociopaths
To dart, in the iridescence of their benevolence.

Late

All you recall of this a.m.'s interrupted dream
Is that you were late,
That you missed the train, for an abundance of chaos,
The train that should have extricated you
From metastasizing lies circling your destiny
Or from the skewering tusk of a narwhal-locomotive
Screaming down the tracks, toward where you waited —

A station crowded with thousands of dilatory spirits,
Who, like you, had misplaced their fates,
Arrived hours, days, generations too late
To climb aboard the last passenger express to freedom,
That narwhal a shabby phantom,
Chuff-chuffing all of you, from the *Umschlagplatz*,
To an unknown depot beyond your souls.

Now that you've been awake for three or four hours
(Months? years? decades?),
You find that that black steam engine,
Its cars stuffed to the guts, like *Blutwurst* links,
Keeps running with the rising sun,
Its lengthening shadow your own,
Forever receding from your departed dream.

An Exceptional Night on the Graveyard Shift

One night, night simply never arrived.
It wasn't that you'd died, that you were dead,
Or anything quite so dire and final as that.

Indeed not! No, sirree! To be sure!
It was nothing of the kind,
Just some phenomenological glitch in the atmosphere,

A leap-evening, you might say, a hole in time,
Twelve nonexistent hours
Falling through the cracks, devoured by voracious space.

And, really, that was all there was to that,
With one easily overlooked exception:
The 5:40 Friday morning

Upon which you assumed you'd be awakening,
To shower, shave, dress, prepare your head for work,
Was, in fact, 5:40 Thursday afternoon,

When you'd driven home, after a bad day at the factory,
Microwaved sweetbreads, headcheese,
Fried rice, meat loaf, bratwurst, mashed potatoes,

Plopped down on the sofa, with a glass of Liebfraumilch,
To catch an hour or two of reality TV
Or an episode of *Desperate Hausfraus*,

Before throwing off your jackboots and soiled uniform,
Hurling your exhausted body into bed,
For a necessary refresher,

Prior to the 5:40 morning alarm calling you to attention,
Only to have you realize that night never arrived,
Rather shortchanged you, stiffed you,

Left your tired existence holding the bag,
Begging for sleep, as, for all intents and purposes,
You'd arrived home, just in time to turn right around,

Head back to the death factory,
To resume inspecting which dolls would pass
And which would be tossed into the incinerators.

The Ravine

Heading home, this late, gray afternoon,
From wherever you're just coming,
Toward which you must, or at least might, be going,

You peer into a sheer ravine of memories,
See crushed, blood-encrusted bones,
And nearly recognize a vague simulacrum of yourself,

Or what, not so long ago,
Might have passed for the skeleton of your soul,
Hiding in a primordial forest.

You'd like to descend into that abyss,
Though you know it's bottomless, dimensionless,
Perhaps find an answer to the Jewish Question.

But you deem it best to keep pressing ahead,
Just in case where you could be going
Might lead you back from some point of no return.

II: LUNACY

Mein Kampf, by Satan

Once, just once,
An aspiring writer set himself the spiritual task
Of composing an entire *Paradise Lost* in forty-two lines.

He began by invoking his muse, a common prostitute,
To give him the balls to pen a work of art
Befitting John Milton, which she did,

Albeit not without exacting a heady surcharge:
Ten dozen eggs, eight sides of beef, dental floss,
And a robust fuck, five nights a week, for eternity.

Then he brought himself onstage, disguised as a snake,
Along with an innocent lady capable of mendacious ways
And a helpmate too strait-laced for his own good.

Next, he introduced three hithertofore unspoken concepts —
Innocence, forbidden fruit, disobedience —
And created an environment of stress, conflict, and mistrust.

Finally, he set in motion a scheme of circumstances
By which he, the fallen viper of paradise,
Directed mankind's ignorant prototypes

In a morality play worthy of his most abysmal demons,
Ending with his two stars being ejected from Eden,
Wandering, hand in hand, through inhospitable lands,

Until they reached, untold generations later,
The sacred purlieus of the millennial Third Reich,
Where their hapless offspring, indefensible Jewish souls,

Adams and Eves a billion times removed
From Avram and Hagar/Sarai,
Were gassed and burned in hellish crematoriums,

Cast into the heavens, through roaring chimney stacks.
Then it was over, all over. Paradise was lost.
The playwright was shorn of his stunted upper-lip mustache,

Shot in the cranium, by his faithful mistress, Eve Braun.
Her earthly consort, Adam Schicklgruber,
Died, beyond Auschwitz, beyond the land of Sobibor,

In the stinking, lice-ridden precincts of Nod,
That rat-infested ghetto the snake promised them
When first they fell from his grace.

After all was said and done
And the morality play, dramatizing right and wrong,
Turned its last page, drew the curtain on its stage,

Nothing much was left of the aspiring writer
Except his twisted molted skin,
Spelling out *"Judenrein."*

The Poet Who Wrote Free-Verse Tattoos

One vile night,
You tried to hide inside yourself,
Elude the parasites that had been biting your mind.

You lay low in the bomb shelter of your soul,
Located below the *Umschlagplatz*,
Through which once passed your imagination's soldiers,

Coming from and going to the wars,
The wars you fought against the crooked cross,
That four-bladed scythe that winnowed the lands.

But eluding your demons was impossible,
Even that deep in the recesses of intellect's forgetting.
They routed you out, naked, cowering, cold,

A disgraced old goat, far gone in your cups,
Incapable of defending yourself,
A slobbering, doddering fool, crawling on all fours,

Reciting unrecognizable rhymes,
Untranslatable growls predating Neanderthals, apes,
God.

When the fiends were finally done with you
And dumped you in a camp for rampant madmen,
You froze in its desert of burning oceans.

And there, in solitude, you died,
Scribbling poetic tattoos across death's flesh,
Trying to leave behind clues to the truth of the lies.

Candle

Nothing could be uglier than evil,
But evil couldn't hold a candle to the Satan beetle
Eating itself.

And the Satan beetle couldn't hold a candle
To Hitler's death's-head asp
Consuming Jews.

The Black Attic

One boring morning,
You lowered the trapdoor in the ceiling of your brain
And began climbing its rickety ladder.

Each rung seemed a month apart,
And by the time you reached the stifling black attic,
Memory had left you for dead.

Thank God that before forgetting erased your slate,
You'd remembered to bring along a flashlight.
The darkness was crowded with indiscernible objects,

Which, under the scrutiny of your four-watt bulb,
Disclosed themselves to be corpses
Hanging from hooks tied to Piranesian ropes and chains

Dangling from the starry vault of heaven —
Souls in various stages of transit from one zone to another,
Along the railroad running between Death and Forever.

Before your flashlight faltered, sputtered out,
You almost recognized yourself amidst the thousands
Waiting to be loaded onto the trains,

But you weren't completely certain.
You looked so different from what you couldn't recall
Of that life below the brain's trapdoor,

Where, once upon a not-so-happily-ever-after,
You existed by your wisdom and wits.
Eventually, your eyes accommodated to the black attic.

III
Perished

Tonight, You Sleep

Was it the flick of the dice or a magician's trick?
Was it the night the glass shattered
Or the start of the plagues from Moses' dreams?

You would never know,
So inept were your powers of divination,
To discern the slightest formulations of cosmic change.

And yet, you suspected something had come to pass,
When they made you take off all your clothes,
Walk in front of the hole you'd just dug,

As you shivered, urinated, shat from pure fear,
Before the machine guns rattled, snorted, roared,
Ripped your guts, shredded your other organs,

Thrust you into a pit of bloody, writhing silence,
For your sins against the Aryan race.
Tonight, you sleep, with Abraham, Isaac, and Jacob.

Hindsight

As fast as the hydrogen gas in the *Hindenburg* exploded,
While that vast zeppelin was dropping its ropes,
To land at a mooring mast in America,

That's exactly how fast my life-force escaped me,
When I died, a year later, in Berlin, during Kristallnacht —
My bloodied German citizenship null and void.

Perhaps I should have anticipated such disenfranchisement,
Estrangement from the grudgingly tolerant society
Into which I believed I'd assimilated . . . but I didn't.

Now, in this strange, vaporous twilight hindsight of mine,
I realize that the *Hindenburg* contained enough *Giftgas*
To exterminate six million Jews . . . which it did.

The Deep

For far too many years,
You let the demons of your dysfunctional solitude
Bury you in a ravine, crevasse, abysmal pit of damnation

(A Babi Yar of your own passive making),
Marginalize, segregate, relegate, ghettoize you,
In a place where even your heart refused to go,

The loneliest depot known to the lowliest of mankind,
That death camp to which blasted emotions were sent,
In animal transports hauled by swastika-locomotives,

On the coldest, most feverish nights of civilization,
When every devil, from grisly prehistory,
Through the Dark and Middle Ages, the Renaissance,

All the way to prenuclear modernity,
Gathered outside Berlin, at the ritual *mikvah*s at Wannsee,
To resolve the Jewish question, with a Final Solution —

Euphemisms so colossal, in their disdainful arrogance,
That even the proto- and classical gods, not to mention God,
Quaked, with horror, envisioning Armageddon . . .

Until, ultimately, in an utterly inexplicable paroxysm,
You rose from the stack above your Topf & Söhne manger,
High over Auschwitz's meat-packing crèche,

And exploded into gaseous ashes
That floated all the way back to Babi Yar,
Into which they rained, trying to hide the dead,

Almost as if, in an act of contrition, expiation,
Saying, "What you did to me, to us six million,
Was not only OK but necessary,"

Saying that convoluted logic, misanthropy, psychosis, evil
Are the rules, not the perverse, obscene exceptions,
And that hubris, gratuitous cruelty, hatred incarnate

Are the mandates by which man's future will be judged,
When the beginning comes around, once again,
To return us all to the dark face of the deep.

Surviving Nightmare

It was something about a forest,
A forest in the shape of an upheaved dream,
A forest or a roaring furnace . . . you weren't certain.

The farther you groped your way into that dark abyss
(Abyss or labyrinth of catacombs —
You couldn't tell, for the rotting corpses you could only smell),

The more disconcerted your uncertainty grew,
Until forest and furnace and corpse-choked abyss
Became a visceral force, drawing you into its core.

Upon awakening, next morning,
Whoever you'd been the night before had evaporated.
What had been a mass of organs, muscles, and bones

Was a ravine of burned leaves, sticks, and grass —
Ashes surrounded by an Einsatzgruppen of crows,
Jackdaws blending into the blackness, cawing ferociously,

The birds regurgitating pieces of your soul,
Chunks they'd pecked off and gnawed as dawn rose,
Filling the bleeding forest with a thousand-year night.

III: PERISHED

Pinching Myself

Tonight, I pinch my arm, pinch my toes,
Pinch my tongue, my hips, my gonads, my ass,
Pinch myself in my soul's solar plexus,

Just to prove to myself that I'm a living entity,
A three-dimensional creature
Capable of breathing, consuming, defecating, loving, hating,

A relatively reasonable being,
Wired, sufficiently, with my DNA's neurological circuitry,
To withstand the cyclical rigors of life *and* death.

Tonight, I pinch my elbows, squeeze my cheeks,
Pull my thumb, as discreetly as possible, out of my butt,
Zip my fly, after tucking in my severed *schwanz*,

In hope of reassuring my psyche
That I'm not just an adventitious fly-by-night
But a flesh-blood-and-bone specter of pogrom golems,

Still floating, hovering, looming on humanity's horizon,
Refusing to give up that *Giftgas*sed ghost,
Despite some mustachioed embodiment of evil saying I must,

In a barbaric time of jackbooted Neanderthals,
When one *Heil Hitler* could dispatch entire communities,
Send cesspools of "Jew vermin" to the gas, the furnaces,

Just because they didn't know how to pinch their elbows,
To prove they were still alive,
Say no to the too-persuasive Germanic command

Not to pinch their arms, toes, tongues, hips, gonads, asses,
Their souls' solar plexuses,
Just before succumbing to dying's ultimate *auf Wiedersehen*.

Tonight, I ponder why I'm yet alive,
Despite the Final Solution's appropriation of my pinched bones.
All I can say is this: kill me again, if you must.

Everyjew

One sweltering day,
A hole of colossal proportions got in his way,
Trapped him in its vast cavity, refused to free him.

And there he languished, for the duration of his existence,
Conspiring, with the unaspiring fates,
To escape the clutches of the insatiable enemy.

But he never did dig a tunnel out of his soul,
Rather malingered, chanting songs of sixpence,
Pockets full of wry Falstaffian ribaldry, in his barracks,

Limericks about the gods who conspired with the Nazis,
To send him up the kosher piggies' chimneys,
Into the skies above Poland and Germany,

Where he died, over and over,
In a colossal hole that eternity called Auschwitz,
For lack of a placename even more evil.

III: PERISHED

Pigeon Shit

Nothing, absolutely nothing, I say or do
Is of incontrovertible consequence
Or, in lay terms, holds the slightest sway,
Amidst the panoply of ancient patriarchs,
Or merits the distinction of pigeon shit on a sidewalk.

Indeed, nothing qualifies as an effective catalyst
For justifying the rest of an unbidden life
I hoped had been conceived
To accomplish grand and noble deeds of charity,
Devout sacrifices to man's impoverished spirit,

When, indeed (again that elusively operative word),
All I could really try to accomplish
Was to find a place, in an uncompromising society,
For a pariah Jew to assimilate, endure, survive, exist,
In the years of the Nazi annihilation of *Untermenschen*.

But nothing of the sort formulated itself into order,
When Adolf Hitler became chancellor, in '33,
Assumed power from President Paul von Hindenburg,
Pretended to execute the august duties of state,
With hardly a stutter or a goose-step in his procession.

What, in truth, transpired is this, I dutifully report:
Without a blink of the eye, I died in the fires of Auschwitz,
Sputtered up a Topf & Söhne oven stack,
As Kaddish ashes scattering into the atmosphere —
Pigeon shit, as, already, I've sadly confessed,

Fecal matter easily erased, in a propulsive Nazi rain,
As I was, by my fully assimilated sister and brother
(Jesus-fearing-Gentile stool pigeons),
Who, having pledged their allegiance to the Final Solution,
Did their part to keep Berlin's sidewalks clean.

Anesthesia

Had he known, had anyone ever told him,
That things would be so pleasant —
As easy as inhaling a sweet anesthesia —
Compared with hiding from the unknown,
Cowering in a chronic state of anxiety,
Terrified of seeing his genealogy end with him,
He'd have surrendered long ago.

Had he known, had anyone ever told him,
How soothing that breeze would be,
Flowing, like a stream, through sleep's dream forest,
Whose trees hid him, in their shadows . . .
Had any of his family told him
That going would be so painless, peaceful, easy,
He'd have surrendered in the beginning.

A Meaning of Life

One night, late,
Deeper than the fathoms of shadowy sleep,
You imagined yourself rising
From the catacumbal ashes of Auschwitz —
A collective specter of reborn European Jewry.

And in your dream of transcendence,
You discovered one of life's myriad meanings:
Death isn't the be-all and end-all of mortality,
Rather the beginning of forever after,
Eternity's Gan Eden, teeming with cosmic poppies.

But when you awakened from memoryless slumber,
Many generations later,
All the victims and perpetrators were gone —
Names safe in their graves, ancestries forgotten.
You were the King David of displaced persons.

Once reality set in,
You discovered that your dream was a traitor,
A co-conspirator, with Hitler,
In a plot to exterminate you and your fellow Jews.
You'd not risen from the dead, after all.

Dark Lovers

Tonight, my psyche is visited, haunted, seduced
By the Hindu goddess of time and change, Kali,
As well as the Greek god of death, Thanatos.

Why this anomalous conflation of mythologies and deities
Has collided with my memories,
I can't begin to tell you, though I desperately want to.

Perhaps it has something to do with the forest fire
That ignited, seventy years ago,
And grotesquely scorched, blackened, all of Europe,

Before banking the last of its human embers,
At Auschwitz, Treblinka, Sobibor, Bergen-Belsen, Chelmno,
So very close to finding the Final Solution . . .

And maybe not. Possibly, my *brain* is on fire,
Alive to some new influence capable of changing its mind,
So that it might discover its own solution, to time.

Could it be that the Holocaust never really happened,
That Kali and Thanatos were dark lovers,
Who never seized me, never tattooed me, never burned me?

He and You

Then, one day (or was it a night?),
Out of the clear blue, the scintillant thin air,
He awakened from life, as if from a dreamless dream,

Into the perpetual reality of nowhere everywhere — eternity —
Death's place in the sun,
At the right hand of the One, the Son,

The Being of Incalculable Light,
Whose salvific rays absolve the measureless days and nights
Of hypothermia, melanoma — malaises common to man.

And there, in that brilliant essence of breathless forever,
He realized he was you
And that you had no clue as to the nature of your uprooting,

Not the slightest insight into the reason for your freedom,
Your unanticipated liberation from flesh and bones —
A case of mortal miscalculation,

A mere accident of skewed depth perception,
Which, instantaneously, turned into an invitation, from death,
To join the rush toward oblivion.

And then it was over . . . all the funereal fuss.
You were dead to the world, just like that,
A dead issue, you might say,

An absented presence, an evanescent putrescence
Moldering in your pit, a disembodied *he*,
An incorporeal *you*, wearing anonymity's identity tattoo,

Just as you did in your *Lager* days and nights,
Your earthly eternities as an Auschwitz-Birkenau ghost,
When time was told in numbers climbing your left forearm,

Climbing, Nazarene-like, in blue-tattoo numerals,
Climbing up your spine,
Climbing down from your Jewish crucifix,

To the base of your nonexistence,
Out of the clear blue of your tattooed numerals, into the light,
The light of the thousand-year Reich,

One of the six million martyrs to the cause of Aryan purity,
You/he an insignificant, ephemeral human being,
Too inconsequential to count,

To count the numerals rising, like a chimney stack,
Up your left forearm, into the sky,
Belching the acrid ashes of your immaculate humanity,

Until the beginning and the end were indistinguishable
And the he/you and the you/he merged into sun and moon,
Chasing each other through eternity.

Beyond Sleep

Night after night, perpetually,
His dreams drag him down, to the depths of despair,
Force him to forgo sleep, as he fights off demons
That would keep him from surfacing,
Dragging his weary spirit up, from the chasm of shadows,
Back into dawn's dishwater light —
Goose-stepping jackboots that trample him yet.

Why doesn't the cacophony of those infernal dreams
Ever go silent,
Let him rest, leave him in provisional peace,
At least for an evening or two, a week, forever,
Abandon him, for more consequential prey —
Jews who escaped the net, refuse to forget?
After all, why keep beating a dead horse to death?

I Did

In a distance, a vast absence,
At once as indiscernible and familiar as yesterday,
I fell prey to something approximating paranoia

(A hazy shape, an amorphous simulacrum?),
Fell into a deep state of enervation,
Fell, face-first, into a slough of desperation

(A strange glow emanating from a train station?),
Fell for Satan's promise of salvation,
Fell from grace, into eternally burning damnation

(The demon stalking my soul's synagogue?),
Fell, headlong, into a ravine, an ossuary,
Fell into lockstep with death

(An effigy, vague acquaintance of mine?).
In a distance, a vast absence,
Yesterday invited me to stay the night. I did.

The Pattern

This disconsolate night,
I'm fading into the pattern of my shadow's anonymity,
Withdrawing into its dreary crevasse —
A rift crowded with human ash —
Disappearing into the death of my very presence.

The freefalling feeling of being totally alone,
So alone that I don't even recognize my voice, my shape,
Is a sensation I've not known, for seven decades.
It's dreadful when solitude hovers over you,
Like a buzzard circling on a spectral thermal,

And you can see that you've already gone over the edge,
Succumbed to time's talons, beak,
Been sucked earthward, crashed into a ravine,
That ineradicable gash history has named Babi Yar,
In which your nameless shadow hasn't even a past.

Haven't Yet

"Ephemeral," "evanescent," "brief" —
Adjectives that understudy for the same idea:
Gikh, *schnell* . . . Endlösung.

But why should I give two hoots in hell?
I mean, what difference does any of this make to me?
All I know is that haste makes waste.

Furthermore, the last thing I'm in is a hurry.
At the ripe old early age of twenty-five,
I learned that I'd never die.

And do you know what? I haven't yet.
The modern world of iPods, cell phones, computers
May be unable to catch up with its soul,

But I can keep up with mine. I still write longhand —
Letters, checks, legal briefs, diary entries —
Still type my treatises, on a Mercedes manual.

That I'm in this for the long haul, taking it slow,
Comes as no surprise to the ancient patriarchs,
Who regulate my eternal pacemaker.

They, more than most,
Appreciate my refusal to measure time in millenniums,
Encourage me to bad-mouth death,

Revel in my disregard for the hazards of the heart,
The inconveniences of mortality,
Remind me that life is the matrix of *forever*.

Once upon a grotesque Third Reich ago,
The sovereignty of my Juden spirit
Was, in the rap on a door, horrifically ripped from me.

That was sixty-five years before tonight,
When, inside a hissing shower,
Adonai promised I wouldn't die. I haven't yet.

IV
These Days

Experiments

Sometime within the past month,
I perused, parsed, then mentally filed away
An article disclosing the cruelty to chimpanzees

The National Institute of Allergy and Infectious Diseases
Has been perpetrating, by extracting their bone marrow,
Using them as surrogate-human incubators,

To produce antibodies for anthrax and smallpox,
At grievous fear and pain to these intelligent, social creatures,
Keeping many caged, in dire isolation, for up to twenty years.

The more gruesome details of these experiments,
(Research supposedly crucial for protecting us from bioterrorism,
Though the drugs for these pathogens are already stockpiled),

Cause my moral sensibility to coalesce around my imagination.
I empathize with those chimps, as though they're victims
Being subjected to Nazi "medical experiments" —

Atrocities too sadistic to be performed on Germans
But perfect for *Untermensch* Jews,
Inferiors too verminous to be considered people.

Why must my ethical instincts struggle with the Holocaust,
Just when I believed enough years had evaporated
To render my forgetting complete?

And why am I compelled
To equate the molestation of innocent chimpanzees
With the genocide of millions of Europeans,

Feel myself transported, in a black cormorant's beak,
Back to the precipice of apocalyptic despair,
Then plunging a thousand years, through the air?

Could it be that I'm suspicious of anyone in a lab coat
Who claims he's trying to protect his nation
From being defiled?

The Victim Who Survived His Nonexistence

Twice upon a time in and out of time,
He tried to tunnel from the Litzmannstadt ghetto,
But on both frenzied attempts,
He got caught by the mind Gestapo,
Which operated out of his psyche's Reichstag.

How he ended up there to begin with
Was beyond his puny powers to grasp.
Even his fluid imagination hadn't a clue.
Indeed, he wasn't human, let alone Jewish,
Just a creation of a sick *Zeitgeist*.

Though revisionist historians deny his authenticity,
Insist he was never tormented by the Nazis,
He knows he's a genuine survivor,
Despite existing solely in a Shoah poem
Written by a man with no ties to the Holocaust.

These days, he's too old to tunnel,
Too tired to resist dying of typhus, *Giftgas*, or fire,
In order to liberate his soul
From the artifice of the well-meaning poet,
Who would keep him alive for the sake of art.

Holocaust Contest

For more than three eye-blearying hours,
You read submissions, from high schoolers,
To a contest focused on the Holocaust —
Poems and essays, teenagers' sincere attempts
To make sense of hatred, intolerance, and violence,
Derive something redemptive
From an event essentially meaningless.

Oh, those compassionate, hopeful minds,
So open and eager to repair the broken world,
With their naive optimism, innocence,
Their unadulterated faith in God's forgiveness,
Man's capacity to learn from his mistakes,
Their insistence that eleven million people
Couldn't have died for no reason.

Exhausted, drained, you left the readers' room
(Which you'd shared with five teachers,
Infinitely more qualified than you,
A reclusive seventy-five-year-old immigrant poet,
To analyze and pick the best entries)
And turned in your selections.
You'd rated all of them "1"s — no "2"s, "3"s, "4"s.

After all, how could you say no
To any of those students,
Who'd dared to confront that subject matter
(Which the twenty-first century and history itself
Has neatly tied into clichéd bundles,
Stuffed away in dark closets)
And tried to make it part of their heritage?

Driving home, you wept not for your life
But for all those contestants,
Who'd never really know,
From books, movies, and survivors like you,
Who come to their classes,
As living proof of the camps' ravages,
What's it like not to stop wishing you were dead.

Not Enough Information

This morning, I read, in *USA Today*,
An article about souvenirs
Taken aboard Shuttle missions.

I was particularly intrigued
By one example:
A religious scroll that flew on *Columbia*.

I wish I had more information,
To fill in the story at least slightly —
Any pieces that might enlighten.

What did the scroll contain?
The Ten Commandments? A parsha?
Was it in a mezuzah?

The Jewish boy who owned the scroll
Was in a concentration camp.
Did he survive?

Was it a labor or death camp?
Was it in Germany or Poland?
Did he give the scroll to someone else?

If so, why?
How did the scroll get to Israel?
Whose hands did it pass through,

If any, other than the boy's,
To end up with Ilan Ramon,
Israel's first astronaut,

Who took it into space, in 2003,
Aboard *Columbia*,
Brought it along, for good luck,

A symbol of human fortitude
That rose from the ashes of genocide . . .
Exploded in a firestorm —

Spacecraft, crew of seven —
Scattering identifiable pieces
Across four states?

I wish I had more information.
Did anyone recover anything
Resembling a religious scroll?

Oskar Selbstmord

He knew he would,
Just not when or where or why or how, exactly.
No matter that he was short on guts,
A coward to his empty core,
A pusillanimous little piece of anonymity,
He knew he would do it — take his life, that is,
Exterminate himself, by his own allegiance to fate.

Trouble was, guts removed from the equation,
He resolutely refused to take pills
(All his life, he'd distrusted medical science).
Shooting himself was out of the question,
Since he fiercely advocated the eradication of guns.
As for inhaling carbon monoxide in his garage,
He thought Willy Loman was a phony.

When all else failed, what he could rely on,
In making a case for suicide,
Was the Himmler/Eichmann/Hoess legacy,
Which haunted him throughout his late middle-age —
Those naked kikes he'd crowded into showers,
Watching them choke, piss, shit, spasm.
Yesterday, he stabbed himself in the soul.

Monopoly

Call them cattle cars; call them golden chariots;
Call them by any euphemism
Attributable to Nazi subtlety,

And you yet get smacked in the glass jaw,
With reality's lead-filled gloves,
Stung by a Schmeling below-the-belt uppercut.

There is no delicate way, or so they say,
For Germans to wash down the sins of their elders
With Vaterland lager.

Something beyond reckoning affected a whole nation,
Once upon a not-so-long-ago Reich,
Which elevated hatred to the sovereignty of a godhead,

Compelled its frenzied population
To wreak vengeance upon a defenseless people,
Force them into charnel houses,

Bury them there, under their charred bones,
Their heritage's smoldering ashes,
As if the Master Race were proclaiming itself YHWH.

But mortality goes on,
According to Machiavelli, Hobbes, Nietzsche,
Franco, Mussolini, Stalin, Hitler,

And death is just a game of Monopoly,
Its tokens rabbis, phylacteries, Torahs, cattle cars,
Its properties Auschwitz, Treblinka, Dachau . . .

Unpronounceable

One night early in April, about nine,
My wife and I went to dine at a nearby restaurant
And found ourselves mesmerized by the maître d',
Who, as he soon told us,
Had defected from Poland, in 1980.

After he seated us at our favorite table,
I asked him to pronounce John Paul II's name for us,
Then "Oswiecim," which he did.
He repeated the latter twice, adding "Brzezinka"
To that ugliest of words in his vocabulary.

"Talk about unforgettable. That place is haunted.
My father was a geologist; he traveled all over Poland.
When I was fourteen, he took me on one of his trips.
After he finished his work,
We drove sixty miles out of our way, to Oswiecim.

"That was in the '70s. All those people were still there.
I could hear them moaning, screaming, thrashing —
They were there, in the walls, the dirt, the sky."
"Why did your father take you?"
"He wanted to teach me, have me learn about evil."

In less than three minutes,
He'd unloosed deeply suppressed emotions,
For which he became self-consciously apologetic.
We thanked him for sharing something so personal.
Turning away, he seemed relieved.

"Do you think Jacek is Jewish?" my wife asked.
"I doubt it. Do you think he knows we are?"
"What difference does it make?"
We tried to pronounce "Oswiecim" and "Karol Wojtyla"
But kept getting tongue-tied in their contradiction.

Yesterday and Yesterday and Yesterday

Yesterday and yesterday and yesterday
Creep into my petty pace, like aging beggars,
Tatterdemalions trading vague smiles, for tarnished pennies,
With dybbuks, ghosts, phantasms, poltergeists, wraiths,
On streets with neither beginnings nor ends,

And I'm the guy behind the myriad spectral disguises,
The vampire, the zombie, the living-dead somnambulist
Out working the public thoroughfares,
Trying to find a touch of social intercourse, to allay my loneliness,
A spot of reoxygenated blood, to vitalize my heart.

What a strange and altogether otherworldly mortality I lead,
Trying simply to survive my allotted years,
Just get by,
Outlive the opprobrium, the disgrace of being fated to exist
Way beyond the covenant between YHWH and Abraham.

It's the curse of the past, *my* past, that haunts me —
My heritage of enslavement, ghettoization, genocide —
Just because my people, my race, *I* don't belong,
Don't conform, don't fit (never have, never will)
Into that mold labeled "Convert or burn in hell" . . .

That curse of the blood libel,
Perpetrated by protocols of the specious Elders of Zion,
That generational disdain toward the Jew,
Which never exposed Martin Luther for the blatant racist he was —
A predacious wolf in reforming sheep's robes.

Oh, how I bleed, bleed, bluster on, all these centuries later.
The pain from my lacerations, the spikes driven, deeply,
Through my pariah's heart,
Reminds me that yesterday and yesterday and yesterday
Yet creep into my poor, petty, pitiable, pathetic pace,

Begging me to put an honorable end to this sham of an existence,
Which never had a tatterdemalion's chance of succeeding,
Merely a vampiric somnambulist's hope
Of sucking enough blood from the necks of feckless gentiles
To supply fodder for the Jewish tribes, ensure survival.

Nonetheless, here I still am, tonight,
Fighting to stay alive, despite all odds to the contrary,
Wondering what I might conjure, to secure my perpetuity,
In a world that sees Jews as a blight of vermin, excrement,
Conspires, every chance it can, to exterminate its dread enemy,

As yesterday and yesterday and yesterday
Press in on today, on tomorrow, on forever and beyond,
Doing their best to arrest man's basest depredations
Long enough to give evil a rest from itself,
Knowing tarnished pennies buy nothing, especially not time.

Latrine

To be able to retreat, conveniently, hastily, from reality
Is what each of us needs to do
If we're going to find living life the slightest bit hospitable.

Think about it . . . long and hard and deep.
Does anyone consult us, before we're born into this world,
As to whether or not we'd consent to such disruption?

No! Emphatically no!
After all, this business of existence is the lime pits,
And there's hardly any way of getting around it . . . them.

Oh, for sure, there're ropes to learn, strings to pull,
Though most of them turn out to be well connected
To overhead-toilet tanks. No thanks.

Each of us has to grit his ground-down or missing teeth
And, as they say in the cliché racket,
Make the best of a really wretched situation.

When push comes to shove, at the old Auschwitz latrine,
We've got to butt in line, bare it all, in the end,
Preferably not with a shit-eating grin.

So there you have it, in the shell of my guts' nuts
(Or is it my nuts' guts?),
My philosophy on the nature of getting by and through,

In a time of overpopulation, global warming,
Distrust among nations — allies and enemies alike —
My take on the chances of getting out unscathed,

Escaping death's biases, its ethnic and religious hatreds,
Keeping them frozen in forgetting's headlights
Long enough to complete the detour back to paradise.

Short of this, we're screwed and tattooed blue,
Lined up back at Auschwitz-Birkenau-Buna's latrines,
Too weak even to sanctify our brown souls, with lime.

Risen Grace

I suffer tormented days and nights,
When the only notes I can write, on my dark soul's staffs,
Are answerless questions I ask, of *how* and *why* —

The Holocaust, Shoah, Endlösung,
The Nazis, disguised as kind, decent, cultured Germans,
Creating such a *Meisterwerk*.

What manner of symphonic composition
Could have orchestrated so many people out of civility,
Into the pits of social and moral dissonance,

Been tuned to *Befehl ist Befehl* precision,
Cacophonizing human lives, for the sake of art,
With the sustained overtone of Aryan purity?

Thankfully, I have more sanguine nights and days,
When Brahms, Beethoven, and Bach
Transport my torment to a risen grace — forgiveness.

Vacuum

Thursday afternoon, a diminutive lady of eighty-four
Arrived at my office door.
She'd called, two weeks earlier,

Asking if I might give her a little of my "precious time,"
So she could discuss publishing her memoir
Of growing up in Poland; her years in the Lodz ghetto;

Her deportation to Auschwitz (her father died there),
Then to Bergen-Belsen,
Finally to a camp in Salzwedel, Germany,

Where she and hundreds of other Jewesses
Were forced to make munitions,
Before being liberated by the U.S. Army, in April 1945;

Her days in a displaced-persons camp, in Hanover,
Where she met and married her husband,
Before being transported again, this time to America,

To a flourishing new life, in St. Louis . . .
These and so many other episodes she bequeathed me,
In the briefest two hours I've ever breathed.

Why me?, I might have asked; only, I knew why:
She'd read my books of Endlösung poems,
Remarked the authority of their voices, their reality,

Expressed amazement at their verisimilitude,
In light of my disclosure
That I'd lost no family to the Holocaust.

Rather than being flattered, I felt small, irrelevant,
In attempting to explain, to her,
My compulsion for writing those hundreds of poems,

I, whose suffering has been strictly vicarious,
Unlike hers, which bloodies the pages of stories
She's wrenched from memory's flesh and bones.

Having visited for two too-brief annealing hours —
Two lifetimes, really —
She asked me to give her a hug. I embraced her,

Then she was gone.
Yet her going left a palpable vacuum,
Which seemed to pull the breath out of my spirit.

She'd come seeking advice from a fellow writer,
About getting her unfinished memoir into print,
She the incarnation of my poems' *dramatis personae*,

Speaking, to me, for all those misappropriated souls
Who've perished or survive in my imagination.
And in that vacuum, we yet endure.

BIOGRAPHICAL NOTE

Louis Daniel Brodsky was born in St. Louis, Missouri, in 1941, where he graduated from Country Day School, in 1959. After earning a B.A., magna cum laude, at Yale University in 1963, he received an M.A. in English from Washington University in 1967 and an M.A. in Creative Writing from San Francisco State University the following year.

From 1968 to 1987, while continuing to write poetry, he assisted in managing a 350-person men's-clothing factory in Farmington, Missouri, and started one of the Midwest's first factory-outlet apparel chains. From 1980 to 1991, he taught English and creative writing, part-time, at Mineral Area College, in nearby Flat River. Since 1987, he has lived in St. Louis and devoted himself to composing poems and short fictions. He has a daughter and a son.

Brodsky is the author of eighty-one volumes of poetry (five of which have been published in French, by Éditions Gallimard) and twenty-six volumes of prose, including nine books of scholarship on William Faulkner, and ten books of short fictions, as well as five early unpublished novels, a book of short stories, and a memoir. His poems and essays have appeared in *Harper's*, *Faulkner Journal*, *Southern Review*, *Texas Quarterly*, *National Forum*, *American Scholar*, *Studies in Bibliography*, *Kansas Quarterly*, *Forum*, *Cimarron Review*, and *Literary Review*, as well as in *Ariel*, *Acumen*, *Orbis*, *New Welsh Review*, *Dalhousie Review*, *Poetry New Zealand*, and other journals. His work has also been printed in five editions of the *Anthology of Magazine Verse and Yearbook of American Poetry*.

Brodsky's *You Can't Go Back, Exactly* won the Center for Great Lakes Culture's (Michigan State University) 2004 best book of poetry award.

Brodsky's Website is http://www.louisdanielbrodsky.com.

OTHER POETRY AND SHORT FICTIONS AVAILABLE FROM TIME BEING BOOKS

Yakov Azriel
Beads for the Messiah's Bride: Poems on Leviticus
In the Shadow of a Burning Bush: Poems on Exodus
Swimming in Moses' Well: Poems on Numbers
Threads from a Coat of Many Colors: Poems on Genesis

Edward Boccia
No Matter How Good the Light Is: Poems by a Painter

Louis Daniel Brodsky
At Dock's End: Poems of Lake Nebagamon, Volume Two
At Shore's Border: Poems of Lake Nebagamon, Volume Three
At Water's Edge: Poems of Lake Nebagamon, Volume One
By Leaps and Bounds: Volume Two of *The Seasons of Youth*
The Capital Café: Poems of Redneck, U.S.A.
Catchin' the Drift o' the Draft *(short fictions)*
Combing Florida's Shores: Poems of Two Lifetimes
The Complete Poems of Louis Daniel Brodsky: Volumes One–Four
Dine-Rite: Breakfast Poems
Disappearing in Mississippi Latitudes: Volume Two of *A Mississippi Trilogy*
Eying Widening Horizons: Volume Five of *The Seasons of Youth*
The Eleventh Lost Tribe: Poems of the Holocaust
Falling from Heaven: Holocaust Poems of a Jew and a Gentile *(Brodsky and Heyen)*
Forever, for Now: Poems for a Later Love
Four and Twenty Blackbirds Soaring
Gestapo Crows: Holocaust Poems
Getting to Unknow the Neighbors *(short fictions)*
A Gleam in the Eye: Volume One of *The Seasons of Youth*
Hopgrassers and Flutterbies: Volume Four of *The Seasons of Youth*
Just Ours: Love Passages with Linda, Volume One
Leaky Tubs *(short fictions)*
Mississippi Vistas: Volume One of *A Mississippi Trilogy*
Mistress Mississippi: Volume Three of *A Mississippi Trilogy*
Nuts to You! *(short fictions)*
Once upon a Small-Town Time: Poems of America's Heartland
Our Time: Love Passages with Linda, Volume Two
Paper-Whites for Lady Jane: Poems of a Midlife Love Affair
Peddler on the Road: Days in the Life of Willy Sypher
Pigskinizations *(short fictions)*
Rabbi Auschwitz: Poems of the Shoah
Rated Xmas *(short fictions)*
Saul and Charlotte: Poems Commemorating a Father and Mother

866-840-4334
HTTP://WWW.TIMEBEING.COM

Louis Daniel Brodsky (continued)
Seizing the Sun and Moon: Volume Three of *The Seasons of Youth*
Shadow War: A Poetic Chronicle of September 11 and Beyond, Volumes One–Five
Showdown with a Cactus: Poems Chronicling the Prickly Struggle Between the Forces of Dubya-ness and Enlightenment, 2003–2006
Still Wandering in the Wilderness: Poems of the Jewish Diaspora
The Swastika Clock: Holocaust Poems
This Here's a Merica *(short fictions)*
The Thorough Earth
Three Early Books of Poems by Louis Daniel Brodsky, 1967–1969: *The Easy Philosopher*, *"A Hard Coming of It" and Other Poems*, and *The Foul Rag-and-Bone Shop*
Toward the Torah, Soaring: Poems of the Renascence of Faith
A Transcendental Almanac: Poems of Nature
Voice Within the Void: Poems of *Homo supinus*
With One Foot in the Butterfly Farm *(short fictions)*
The World Waiting to Be: Poems About the Creative Process
Yellow Bricks *(short fictions)*
You Can't Go Back, Exactly

Harry James Cargas (editor)
Telling the Tale: A Tribute to Elie Wiesel on the Occasion of His 65th Birthday — Essays, Reflections, and Poems

Judith Chalmer
Out of History's Junk Jar: Poems of a Mixed Inheritance

Gerald Early
How the War in the Streets Is Won: Poems on the Quest of Love and Faith

Gary Fincke
Blood Ties: Working-Class Poems
Reviving the Dead

Charles Adès Fishman
Blood to Remember: American Poets on the Holocaust *(editor)*
Chopin's Piano
In the Path of Lightning

CB Follett
Hold and Release
One Bird Falling

866-840-4334
HTTP://WWW.TIMEBEING.COM

Albert Goldbarth
A Lineage of Ragpickers, Songpluckers, Elegiasts & Jewelers: Selected Poems of Jewish Family Life, 1973–1995

Robert Hamblin
Crossroads: Poems of a Mississippi Childhood
From the Ground Up: Poems of One Southerner's Passage to Adulthood
Keeping Score: Sports Poems for Every Season

David Herrle
Abyssinia, Jill Rush

William Heyen
Erika: Poems of the Holocaust
Falling from Heaven: Holocaust Poems of a Jew and a Gentile *(Brodsky and Heyen)*
The Host: Selected Poems, 1965–1990
Pterodactyl Rose: Poems of Ecology
Ribbons: The Gulf War — A Poem

Ted Hirschfield
German Requiem: Poems of the War and the Atonement of a Third Reich Child

Virginia V. James Hlavsa
Waking October Leaves: Reanimations by a Small-Town Girl

Rodger Kamenetz
The Missing Jew: New and Selected Poems
Stuck: Poems Midlife

Norbert Krapf
Blue-Eyed Grass: Poems of Germany
Looking for God's Country
Somewhere in Southern Indiana: Poems of Midwestern Origins

Adrian C. Louis
Blood Thirsty Savages

Leo Luke Marcello
Nothing Grows in One Place Forever: Poems of a Sicilian American

866-840-4334
HTTP://WWW.TIMEBEING.COM

Gardner McFall
The Pilot's Daughter
Russian Tortoise

Joseph Meredith
Hunter's Moon: Poems from Boyhood to Manhood
Inclinations of the Heart

Ben Milder
From Adolescence to Senescence: A Life in Light Verse
The Good Book Also Says . . . : Numerous Humorous Poems Inspired by the New Testament
The Good Book Says . . . : Light Verse to Illuminate the Old Testament
Love Is Funny, Love Is Sad
What's So Funny About the Golden Years
The Zoo You Never Gnu: A Mad Menagerie of Bizarre Beasts and Birds

Charles Muñoz
Fragments of a Myth: Modern Poems on Ancient Themes

Brenda Marie Osbey
History and Other Poems

Micheal O'Siadhail
The Gossamer Wall: Poems in Witness to the Holocaust

Charles Rammelkamp
Fūsen Bakudan: Poems of Altruism and Tragedy in Wartime

Joseph Stanton
A Field Guide to the Wildlife of Suburban Oʻahu
Imaginary Museum: Poems on Art

Susan Terris
Contrariwise